MONSTER FIGHT CLUB
DINOSAURS

ANITA GANERI AND DAVID WEST

PowerKiDS
press

New York

Published in 2012 by The Rosen Publishing Group, Inc.
29 East 21st Street, New York, NY 10010

Designed and produced by
David West Books

Designer and illustrator: David West
Editor: Ronne Randall
U.S. Editor: Kara Murray

Photographic credits: 6-7, Kabacchi; 10, mmechtley; 11, jjsala; 14, Kevin Walsh; 18, Kabacchi; 19, Ryan Somma; 22, I, Laikayiu; 23, Bob Ainsworth; 26-27, Kabacchi.

Library of Congress Cataloging-in-Publication Data

Ganeri, Anita, 1961–
Dinosaurs / by Anita Ganeri and David West.
p. cm. — (Monster fight club)
Includes index.
ISBN 978-1-4488-5201-7 (library binding) — ISBN 978-1-4488-5240-6 (pbk.) —
ISBN 978-1-4488-5241-3 (6-pack)
1. Dinosaurs—Juvenile literature. I. West, David, 1956– II. Title. III. Series.

QE861.5.G36 2012
567.9—dc22

2011009829

Manufactured in China

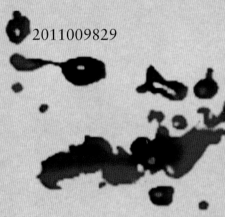

CPSIA Compliance Information: Batch #DS1102PK:
For Further Information contact Rosen Publishing, New York,
New York at 1-800-237-9932

CONTENTS

INTRODUCTION

Welcome to the Monster Fight Club! Watch in amazement as dramatic dinosaurs enter the ring to do battle. Have you ever wondered who would win—a terrible Tyrannosaurus or a spine-chilling Spinosaurus? Find out as you enter their petrifying world.

How Does It Work?

There are six monster fights in this book. Before each fight, you will see a profile page for each contestant. This page gives you more information about them. Once you have read the profile pages, you might be able to take a better guess at who will win the fight.

Supporting illustrations give background information on the fossil finds and other characteristics of the dinosaurs.

WARNING

Blood will be spilled!

The profile pages are crammed with fascinating and bloodcurdling facts about each of the contestants.

A globe shows where their fossils were found, along with information showing the dinosaur's name, the meaning of the name, and when it lived.

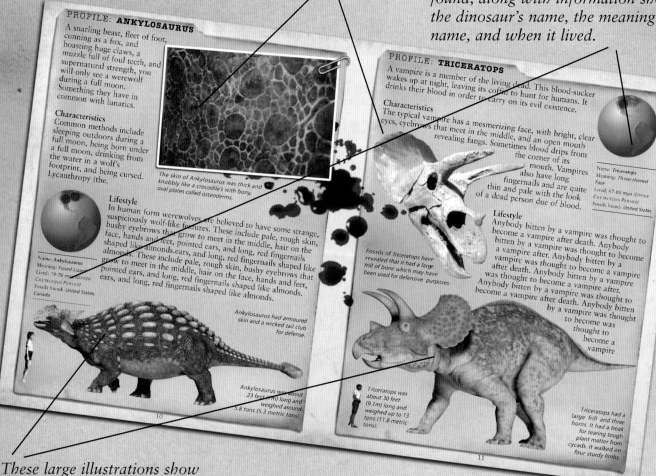

PROFILE: ANKYLOSAURUS

A snarling beast, fleet of foot, cunning as a fox, and boasting huge claws, a muzzle full of foul teeth, and supernatural strength, you will only see a werewolf during a full moon. Something they have in common with lunatics.

Characteristics
Common methods include sleeping outdoors during a full moon, being born under a full moon, drinking from the water in a wolf's footprint, and being cursed. Lycanthropy (the.

The skin of Ankylosaurus was thick and knobbly like a crocodile's with bony oval plates called osteoderms.

Lifestyle
In human form werewolves are believed to have some strange, suspiciously wolf-like features. These include pale, rough skin, bushy eyebrows that grow to meet in the middle, hair on the face, hands and feet, pointed ears, and long, red fingernails shaped like almonds. ears, and long, red fingernails shaped like almonds. These include pale, rough skin, bushy eyebrows that grow to meet in the middle, hair on the face, hands and feet, pointed ears, and long, red fingernails shaped like almonds. ears, and long, red fingernails shaped like almonds.

Name: *Ankylosaurus*
Meaning: *Fused Lizard*
Lived: *74-76 mya (UPPER CRETACEOUS PERIOD)*
Fossils found: *United States, Canada*

Ankylosaurus had armoured skin and a wicked tail club for defense.

Ankylosaurus was about 23 feet (7m) long and weighed around 5.8 tons (5.3 metric tons).

10

PROFILE: TRICERATOPS

A vampire is a member of the living dead. This blood-sucker wakes up at night, leaving its coffin to hunt for humans. It drinks their blood in order to carry on its evil existence.

Characteristics
The typical vampire has a mesmerizing face, with bright, clear eyes, eyebrows that meet in the middle, and an open mouth revealing fangs. Sometimes blood drips from the corner of its mouth. Vampires also have long fingernails and are quite thin and pale with the look of a dead person due of blood.

Name: *Triceratops*
Meaning: *Three-Horned Face*
Lived: *67-65 mya (UPPER CRETACEOUS PERIOD)*
Fossils found: *United States*

Lifestyle
Anybody bitten by a vampire was thought to become a vampire after death. Anybody bitten by a vampire was thought to become a vampire after. Anybody bitten by a vampire was thought to become a vampire after death. Anybody bitten by a vampire was thought to become a vampire after. Anybody bitten by a vampire was thought to become a vampire after death. Anybody bitten by a vampire was thought to become was thought to become a vampire

Fossils of Triceratops have revealed that it had a large frill of bone which may have been used for defensive purposes.

Triceratops was about 30 feet (9.1m) long and weighed up to 13 tons (11.8 metric tons).

Triceratops had a large frill and three horns. It had a beak for tearing tough plant matter from cycads. It walked on four sturdy limbs.

11

These large illustrations show you each contestant, warts and all, to give you a good idea of their physical features.

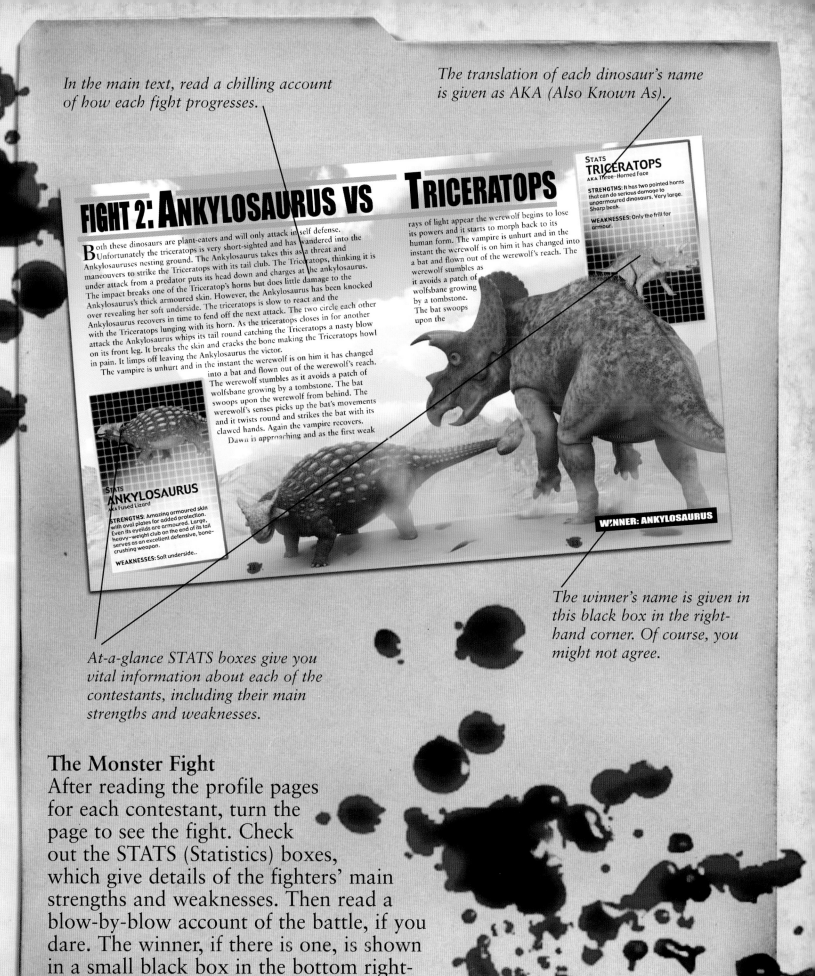

In the main text, read a chilling account of how each fight progresses.

The translation of each dinosaur's name is given as AKA (Also Known As).

FIGHT 2: ANKYLOSAURUS VS TRICERATOPS

STATS
TRICERATOPS
AKA Three-Horned Face

STRENGTHS: It has two pointed horns that can do serious damage to unarmoured dinosaurs. Very large. Sharp beak.

WEAKNESSES: Only the frill for armour.

Both these dinosaurs are plant-eaters and will only attack in self defense. Unfortunately the triceratops is very short-sighted and has wandered into the Ankylosauruses nesting ground. The Ankylosaurus takes this as a threat and maneouvers to strike the Triceratops with its tail club. The Triceratops, thinking it is under attack from a predator puts its head down and charges at the ankylosaurus. The impact breaks one of the Triceratop's horns but does little damage to the Ankylosaurus's thick armoured skin. However, the Ankylosaurus has been knocked over revealing her soft underside. The triceratops is slow to react and the Ankylosaurus recovers in time to fend off the next attack. The two circle each other with the Triceratops lunging with its horn. As the triceratops closes in for another attack the Ankylosaurus whips its tail round catching the Triceratops a nasty blow on its front leg. It breaks the skin and cracks the bone making the Triceratops howl in pain. It limps off leaving the Ankylosaurus the victor.

The vampire is unhurt and in the instant the werewolf is on him it has changed into a bat and flown out of the werewolf's reach. The werewolf stumbles as it avoids a patch of wolfsbane growing by a tombstone. The bat swoops upon the werewolf from behind. The werewolf's senses picks up the bat's movements and it twists round and strikes the bat with its clawed hands. Again the vampire recovers.

Dawn is approaching and as the first weak rays of light appear the werewolf begins to lose its powers and it starts to morph back to its human form. The vampire is unhurt and in the instant the werewolf is on him it has changed into a bat and flown out of the werewolf's reach. The werewolf stumbles as it avoids a patch of wolfsbane growing by a tombstone. The bat swoops upon the

STATS
ANKYLOSAURUS
AKA Fused Lizard

STRENGTHS: Amazing armoured skin with oval plates for added protection. Even its eyelids are armoured. Large, heavy-weight club on the end of its tail serves as an excellent defensive, bone-crushing weapon.

WEAKNESSES: Soft underside..

WINNER: ANKYLOSAURUS

The winner's name is given in this black box in the right-hand corner. Of course, you might not agree.

At-a-glance STATS boxes give you vital information about each of the contestants, including their main strengths and weaknesses.

The Monster Fight
After reading the profile pages for each contestant, turn the page to see the fight. Check out the STATS (Statistics) boxes, which give details of the fighters' main strengths and weaknesses. Then read a blow-by-blow account of the battle, if you dare. The winner, if there is one, is shown in a small black box in the bottom right-hand corner.

PROFILE: THERIZINOSAURUS

Weird! That's what scientists thought when they dug up the first fossils of Therizinosaurus. It was a dinosaur, but not like any dinosaur that they had ever seen before. It was more like a giant turkey with supersized claws. They named it "scythe lizard."

Record Claws

Therizinosaurus's standout features were its claws. At a truly awesome 3 feet (1 meter) long, they were the biggest claws of any animal that has ever lived. Therizinosuaurus's birdlike head was at the end of a long neck, which was attached to its potbellied body.

Name: *Therizinosaurus*
Meaning: *Scythe Lizard*
Lived: 85-70 *mya (UPPER CRETACEOUS PERIOD)*
Fossils found: *Mongolia*

Tree Stripper

Strangely, Therizinosaurus's razor-sharp claws were not used as weapons. Therizinosaurus was probably an herbivore, using its claws to strip leaves from trees and stuff them into its mouth. It might also have ripped apart termite mounds with its claws to scoop out the juicy insects.

Fossils tell us that Therizinosaurus had three giant claws on each hand. The claws were curved, like the blades of a scythe.

Paleontologists think that Therizinosaurus grew up to 26.2 feet (8 m) long, stood 9.8 feet (3 m) tall, and weighed 4 tons (3.6 metric tons).

Nobody has ever found a complete fossil of a Therizinosaurus, but experts think that a Therizinosaurus might have looked like this.

PROFILE: **GIGANTORAPTOR**

Imagine a giant ostrich crossed with a ferocious *Tyrannosaurus rex*! That gives you an idea of the beast that was the terrible Gigantoraptor. Armed with razor-sharp claws and a powerful crushing jaw, Gigantoraptor was more than a match for most other dinosaurs.

Experts reconstructed this Gigantoraptor skeleton from a few pieces of bone found in China in 2007.

One of a Kind

Paleontologists think that Gigantoraptor belonged to a group of dinosaurs called oviraptorsaurs, which were similar to modern birds. But Gigantoraptor was built on a truly gigantic scale and was thirty times heavier than any of its relatives. This one-of-a-kind animal was probably covered with feathers, making it the biggest feathered living thing of all time.

Gigantoraptor stood 16 feet (5 m) tall on two slender legs.

Clawed Hunter

Gigantoraptor was a fast-moving predator. It probably hunted smaller dinosaurs and other animals, but it might also have eaten plants. After ensnaring its prey with its sharp claws, it ripped away its flesh with its sharp, toothless beak— like a monstrous, ravenous vulture.

Name: *Gigantoraptor*
Meaning: *Giant Thief*
Lived: *85 mya (UPPER CRETACEOUS PERIOD)*
Fossils found: *Mongolia, China*

Gigantoraptor measured more than 26 feet (8 m) from its beak to the tip of its tail. It weighed in at about 2.2 tons (2 metric tons).

FIGHT 1: THERIZINOSAURUS VS.

Today's battle takes place on the edge of the Mongolian desert, between two of the strangest dinosaurs ever seen. A Therizinosaurus mother and its youngster are feeding peacefully among the trees. They are unaware that a vicious predator is planning an ambush.

Seizing its chance for a meal, a Gigantoraptor breaks out of the undergrowth and rushes at the young Therizinosaurus. But as it raises its claws to attack, the mother turns and faces it. At first the Gigantoraptor backs off, but then it mounts a ferocious attack on the mother herself. Nimble on its feet, and using its tail for balance, it makes darting runs at the flanks of the Therizinosaurus. With each attack, it lunges at the Therizinosaurus, ripping away flesh with its sharp beak. The Therizinosaurus shrieks in pain. Its youngster looks on in horror. This is not a fair fight. The Therizinosaurus's bulk puts it at a distinct disadvantage. It tries to counterattack, swishing its giant claws. But the agile Gigantoraptor leaps away and mounts yet more attacks of its own. Blood streams from wounds on the Therizinosaurus's neck.

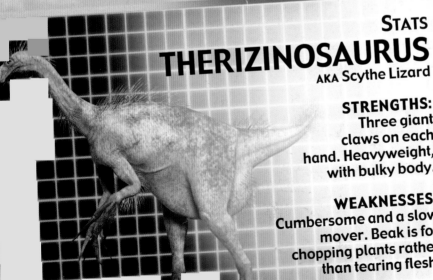

STATS

THERIZINOSAURUS
AKA Scythe Lizard

STRENGTHS: Three giant claws on each hand. Heavyweight, with bulky body.

WEAKNESSES: Cumbersome and a slow mover. Beak is for chopping plants rather than tearing flesh.

GIGANTORAPTUR

Exhausted, and weakened by loss of blood, the Therizinosaurus begins to stumble and sway. Its time is surely up. Sensing victory, the Gigantoraptor comes in for the kill. In a last-ditch effort to defend itself, the Therizinosaurus throws a clawed one-two punch. The raptor avoids the first swipe, but not the second. Claws rip through the soft flesh of its throat. It falls to the ground, arms still flailing. Therizinosaurus is our unlikely winner. But the Gigantoraptor has inflicted mortal wounds, and the victor will die before the day is out.

STATS
GIGANTORAPTOR
AKA Giant Thief

STRENGTHS: Lightweight for its size, making it fast and agile. Sharp claws and beak designed for attack.

WEAKNESSES: For this fight, weighs less than Therizinosaurus. Long, thin neck vulnerable to attack.

WINNER: THERIZINOSAURUS

PROFILE: **ANKYLOSAURUS**

Ankylosaurus was the closest thing to a living tank that ever existed. This whopping plant-eating dinosaur was squat and heavy, like a giant armadillo. And like an armadillo, it was covered with thick, bony armor that protected it from the jaws of its fearsome enemies.

Fused Bones
"Ankylosaurus" means "fused lizard." This dinosaur had weird bony plates on its skin, and these were fused together to make the armor on its neck, back, and tail.

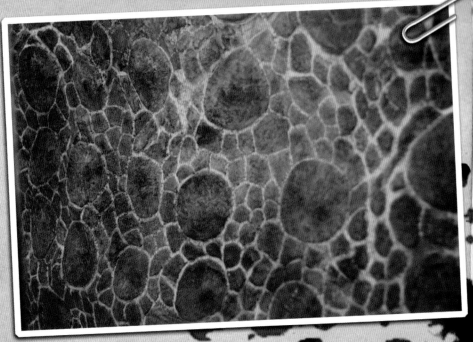

The skin of Ankylosaurus was thick and knobbly, like the skin of a modern crocodile. In the skin were bony plates called osteoderms.

Name: *Ankylosaurus*
Meaning: *Fused Lizard*
Lived: *74-76 mya (UPPER CRETACEOUS PERIOD)*
Fossils found: *United States, Canada*

Spikes and Clubs
Ankylosaurus had other defensive tricks in addition to its armor. Its skull bones were very thick, and bony spikes stuck out from the top of its head to deter attackers. Even its eyelids were armored. At the other end of its body was a weapon it could use for a vicious counterattack. The tip of its long tail formed a heavy club nearly 3 feet (1 m) across. Ankylosaurus used this like a giant sledgehammer, sending it crashing into the legs of attackers with powerful tail muscles.

Ankylosaurus defended itself with a tail club made of enlarged tail bones.

Ankylosaurus was about 23 feet (7 m) long and weighed around 5.8 tons (5.3 metric tons).

PROFILE: **TRICERATOPS**

A pair of giant horns, a super powerful beak, and a big bony frill, all attached to a head more than 6.5 feet (2 m) long. That was Triceratops. It sounds like a terrifying predator, but all it ever preyed on was plants.

A Giant Evolves

Triceratops was one of a group of dinosaurs called ceratopsians. All the ceratopsians had massive heads, with horns and bony frills. They first appeared about 100 million years ago. Early ceratopsians were the size of large dogs, but over millions of years, giant horned dinosaurs evolved. Triceratops was one of the biggest of them all.

Name: *Triceratops*
Meaning: *Three-Horned Face*
Lived: *67-65 mya* (UPPER CRETACEOUS PERIOD)
Fossils found: *United States*

A fossilized Triceratops skull shows the heavy frill it sported behind an enormous, horn-topped head.

Living in Herds

Like modern-day animals such as reindeer and wildebeest, Triceratops lived in large herds. It sliced up tough vegetation with its parrotlike beak, and chewed it with its huge teeth, powered by massive jaw muscles. Triceratops fought off predators with its horns. Its frill may have also have been for protection, keeping its neck safe from the jaws of attackers. Males probably used their horns to grapple with rivals for the top spot in the herd.

Triceratops was about 30 feet (9.1 m) long and weighed as much as 13 tons (11.8 metric tons).

Stocky back legs and a heavy body allowed male Triceratops to withstand attacks from rivals.

FIGHT 2: ANKYLOSAURUS VS.

The scene is the warm, humid plains of North America. The time is 67 million years ago. Our contest brings together two plant-eaters that would normally never attack the other. They only fight when they have to—in self-defense.

Unfortunately, both of these animals suffer from poor eyesight. The Triceratops is particularly nearsighted. Straying from the edge of its herd, it has blundered into the nesting ground of a solitary Ankylosaurus. The Ankylosaurus thinks it is under attack from a predator. But it is too slow to run away, and anyway, it has a nest of precious eggs to defend. It decides to stay put. It turns its back on the Triceratops. This seems like a mistake, but then its plan becomes clear. It is lining up to take a swipe at the Triceratops with its massive tail club. Seeing the Ankylosaurus's club begin to swing, the threatened Triceratops lowers its massive head and charges. The impact makes the ground shake, and causes one of the Triceratops's horns to shatter into pieces. A chunk of bone flies off the Ankylosaurus's back, but its armor is not pierced. It is, however, knocked on its side, revealing its soft underbelly. But before the lumbering Triceratops can attack again, the Ankylosaurus recovers.

The exhausted foes slowly circle each other in the sandy soil. Several times, the Triceratops lunges with its horns, but each time it narrowly misses the Ankylosaurus, which keeps its body close to the ground. Again, the Triceratops moves forward, lifting its head in preparation for

STATS
ANKYLOSAURUS
AKA Fused Lizard

STRENGTHS: Covered with a layer of almost unbreakable armor—even on its eyelids. Massive club on its tail used as a bone-smashing weapon of self-defense.

WEAKNESSES: Slow moving, with a soft underbelly.

TRICERATOPS

another swipe with its horns. This is the chance the Ankylosaurus has been waiting for. It whips its tail around, and its bony club smashes into the Triceratops's leg. Skin is ripped and bones are shattered. The Triceratops howls in pain. Unable to continue the fight, it limps away, leaving the Ankylosaurus the victor.

WINNER: ANKYLOSAURUS

PROFILE: **BRACHIOSAURUS**

Even in the world of monstrous dinosaurs, Brachiosaurus was a giant. Weighing in at 77 tons (as much as 12 African elephants), it was one of the largest animals that has ever lived.

Giant Giraffe
Like a modern giraffe, Brachiosaurus had front legs longer than its back legs (although its legs were very thick to support the animal's massive weight). Its small head was supported on its long, superstrong neck. Its equally long tail balanced its neck and head.

Rumbling Stomach
Brachiosaurus ate the leaves and fruits of conifer trees. It took its pick from the tops of trees, where no other dinosaurs could reach. Its voluminous stomach made low-pitched rumbling noises as it digested half a ton of food at a time.

Name: *Brachiosaurus*
Meaning: *Arm Lizard*
Lived: *155-140 mya (Upper Jurassic/Lower Cretaceous Period)*
Fossils found: *Algeria, Portugal, Tanzania, United States*

Geologist Metrinah Ruzvidzo with a Brachiosaurus's immense femur (thighbone). Some of Brachiosaurus's bones were hollow to reduce its weight.

Brachiosaurus grew up to 82 feet (25 m) long and weighed around 77 tons (70 metric tons). Like other sauropods, it never stopped growing during its life.

PROFILE: **DIPLODOCUS**

An enormously long tail, an enormously long neck, and a tiny head were the features of the amazing Diplodocus. This supersized beast, like the Brachiosaurus (opposite), was one of a group of giant animals called sauropods.

Diplodocus had extra bones along the underside of its tail. The "double-beam" structure of these bones gives the animal its name.

Big Back Bones

Diplodocus was the longest of the sauropods, but it was fairly lightweight compared with its relatives. This was partly because its vertebrae (the bones of its neck, back, and tail) were hollow. Diplodocus's neck and tail contained dozens of bones. There were seventy in the 23-foot-long (7-m) tail alone. These bones had tall spikes where the powerful muscles that supported the neck and tail were attached.

Name: *Diplodocus*
Meaning: *Double Beam*
Lived: *155-145 mya (UPPER JURASSIC PERIOD)*
Fossils found: *United States*

Diplodocus Herds

Diplodocus probably roamed the plains in herds of twenty or more animals, just as elephants do today. This gave them some protection against predators such as the vicious Allosaurus. Diplodocus fed on trees, such as cycads, stripping the upper branches.

This is the skull of a Diplodocus. It is about the size of the skull of a modern horse. The teeth at the front of the jaw stripped leaves from trees.

It may have been able to rear up on its legs and tail to reach as high as possible for food. Diplodocus could crack its tail like a giant whip. It used these cracks, and also stamped the ground, to communicate with other herd members.

When scientists first constructed Diplodocus skeletons, they positioned the head high and the tail dragging along the ground. Today, experts think that the Diplodocus held its neck and tail horizontally to balance each other out.

Diplodocus was about 89 feet (27 m) long and weighed around 24 tons (21.8 metric tons).

FIGHT 3: BRACHIOSAURUS VS.

This is a battle of two truly supersized giants. Brachiosaurus and Diplodocus are two enormous animals. These beasts are placid plant-eaters. Neither boasts an offensive weapon or defensive armor. They normally stay out of trouble. Predators are wary of attacking them because of their size. In fact, Brachiosaurus is so huge that even the deadly Tyrannosaurus steers clear of it.

STATS

DIPLODOCUS
AKA Double Beam

STRENGTHS: Giant size. Long, whiplike tail for defense.

WEAKNESSES: Lightweight compared with Brachiosaurus. No offensive weapons.

STATS

BRACHIOSAURUS
AKA Arm Lizard

STRENGTHS: Super heavyweight—no predators would dare to attack it. Can rear up on its hind legs.

WEAKNESSES: Very slow mover because of weight. No defensive weapons.

Brachiosaurus is stripping the leaves from a group of conifer trees. With its massive weight, it has knocked some of the trees flat to reach the juiciest leaves. But trouble is brewing—a Diplodocus is also on the lookout for food. It has wandered into the group of trees and is munching on one of the fallen conifers. The Brachiosaurus is not very pleased. No intruder is going to steal its tasty lunch. It lumbers toward the Diplodocus.

DIPLODOCUS

Crack! Crack! Crack! The Diplodocus swings rapidly from side to side, creating a series of gunshot sounds with the whiplike tip of its tail. This odd sound makes the Brachiosaurus hesitate, but then it lifts its head to one side and swipes it down, striking the Diplodocus at the base of its neck. The Diplodocus lets out a bellow of pain. Despite more warning cracks from the Diplodocus's tail, the Brachiosaurus advances again. It rears up on its powerful hind legs and then crashes down onto the Diplodocus's back. The ground shudders and shakes. Under the massive bulk of the Brachiosaurus, the Diplodocus collapses. Ribs crack and internal organs are crushed. The stricken beast gasps its last few breaths. Brachiosaurus is the victor.

WINNER: BRACHIOSAURUS

PROFILE: **VELOCIRAPTOR**

A quick, cunning, and ruthless killer with a fearsome reputation—that is Velociraptor. But this dinosaur was no giant monster—it was no taller than a small child. But with razor-sharp teeth and slashing claws, this pint-sized predator packed a very big punch for its size.

Name: *Velociraptor*
Meaning: *Speedy Thief*
Lived: *84-80 mya (UPPER CRETACEOUS)*
Fossils found: *Mongolia*

Fast Runner

Velociraptor looked like a large bird. It stood on its long, slender hind legs. These legs made it agile and quick. It could run at speeds up to 37 miles per hour (60 kph) for short bursts. A long, stiff tail kept it perfectly balanced as it pursued its prey.

Velociraptor had a long head with an upturned snout, and a jaw filled with serrated, backward-pointing teeth.

A Clever Hunter

Velociraptor's name means "speedy thief." It was a fast predator that hunted down small and medium-sized dinosaurs, such as Protoceratops and Hadrosaurus. It also raided nests for dinosaur eggs and ate young dinosaurs. It had a large brain for its size and was fairly intelligent. It hunted in packs, like modern hunting dogs such as hyenas.

Velociraptor had claws like those of a modern bird of prey. The second toe on each foot had a big, sharp claw that could pierce skin easily.

Fossils of Velociraptor show that it was covered with feathers. On its forelimbs were extra-long feathers that were probably used for courtship displays.

Velociraptor grew up to 5.9 feet (1.8 m) long and weighed up to 33 pounds (15 kg).

PROFILE: **PROTOCERATOPS**

Protoceratops was the size of a large pig, and just as heavy. But it was still one of the smaller dinosaurs. Its outstanding feature was the bony frill on its head that covered the back of its neck. The frill was an extension of Protoceratops's skull. It may have been there to protect Protoceratops's neck from predators, but it may also have been designed for showing off during courtship displays.

The skeleton shows the neck frill at the back of its skull. The frill itself contained two large holes, while its cheeks had large protruding bones.

Horned but Hornless

"Protoceratops" means "first horned face." So where is its horn? The answer is that it didn't have one. But it was one of a group of dinosaurs that were forerunners of later, larger horned dinosaurs, such as Triceratops.

Name: *Protoceratops*
Meaning: *First Horned Face*
Lived: *84-80 mya (UPPER CRETACEOUS)*
Fossils found: *Mongolia*

Beak and Teeth

Protoceratops was a plant-eating dinosaur. It bit off mouthfuls of plants with its powerful parrotlike beak and chewed them with teeth in the back of its mouth. Protoceratops lived in herds, and mothers looked after their nests of eggs until they hatched.

Protoceratops was approximately 6 feet (1.8 m) in length and weighed up to 400 pounds (180 kg). A fully-grown specimen stood about 2 feet (0.6 m) high at the shoulder.

FIGHT 4: VELOCIRAPTOR VS

PROTOCERATOPS
AKA First Horned Face

STRENGTHS: Heavy build. Powerful, sharp beak for cropping plants can be used for self-defense.

WEAKNESSES: No armor.

In a sandy desert, a group of ravenous Velociraptors finally find the prey they're looking for—a lone Protoceratops. The Protoceratops is guarding a nest of eggs—the eggs are a bonus for the Velociraptors. The excited predators spread out and surround the Protoceratops. But just as they are about to drive home their attack, a sudden gust of wind ruffles their feathers. Within seconds, the air is thick with dust—a sandstorm has blown up! The Velociraptors lose sight of each other and their intended meal. But one attacker is lucky—by chance it stumbles across the Protoceratops.

The Velociraptor circles the stationary Protoceratops, looking for an opportunity to make the first strike. The Protoceratops makes short charges at the Velociraptor, but the agile Velociraptor easily evades them. Then, suddenly, Velociraptor leaps onto the back of the Protoceratops. It digs the long, daggerlike claws on its feet into the Protoceratops's back. The Protoceratops lets out a horrific squeal. It rolls onto its side in the sand. The Velociraptor leaps to the ground to escape being crushed. Before Protoceratops can recover, Velociraptor attacks again. On one foray, it sinks one of its claws into the Protoceratops's neck, severing a major artery. On the next, it rips a hole in the Protoceratops's windpipe with its teeth. The Protoceratops has no response to this onslaught. Slowly, it weakens from loss of blood and exhaustion, and finally collapses. Velociraptor is the victor. But there's an unexpected twist to this fight. As Velociraptor moves in for the kill, Protoceratops manages to clamp its beak around the Velociraptor's leg, snapping the bones. Velociraptor cannot free itself, and the two foes become buried together as the windblown sand settles over them.

PRUTOCERATUPS

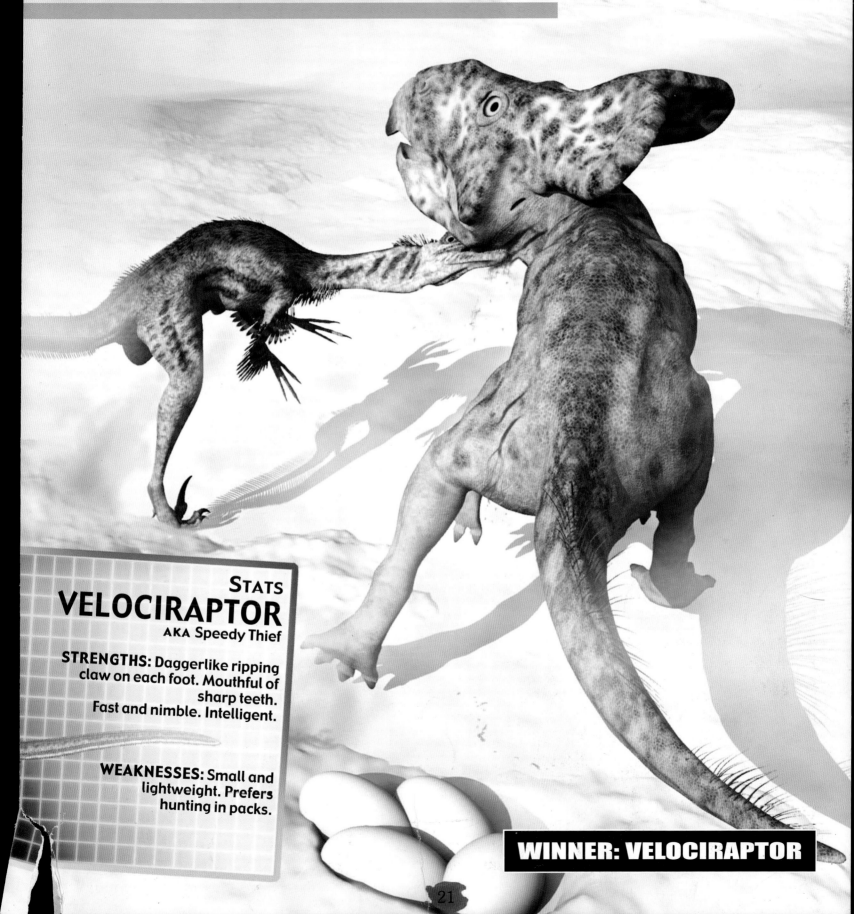

STATS
VELOCIRAPTOR
AKA Speedy Thief

STRENGTHS: Daggerlike ripping claw on each foot. Mouthful of sharp teeth. Fast and nimble. Intelligent.

WEAKNESSES: Small and lightweight. Prefers hunting in packs.

WINNER: VELOCIRAPTOR

PROFILE: **MICRORAPTOR**

A creature you could have held in your hand, Microraptor was one of the tiniest dinosaurs that ever lived. It was also one of the strangest—it looked like a small bird with four wings. It may have been a link between the dinosaurs, long since dead, and the birds of today.

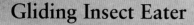

The first fossil of Microraptor was found in China in 2000. Many more fossils have since been found. They show that Microraptor sported feathers.

Name: *Microraptor*
Meaning: *Little Thief*
Lived: *120 mya (Lower Cretaceous)*
Fossils found: *China*

Four Wings

Fossils of Microraptor show that it belonged to a group of dinosaurs called the dromaeosaurs, which walked on two legs. Velociraptor (see page 18) was also a member of the group. But Microraptor was a strange beast. Fossils show that it was covered with small feathers, and had long feathers on its front and rear limbs. The long feathers allowed Microraptor to glide using both sets of legs as simple wings, like a modern flying squirrel.

Gliding Insect Eater

Microraptor may have lived in trees, climbing up using claws on all four of its feet, and gliding from tree to tree. It ate a diet of insects but it might also have hunted on the ground. Many experts believe that modern birds evolved from dinosaurs. Microraptor could have been one of the steps on the road from dinosaurs to birds.

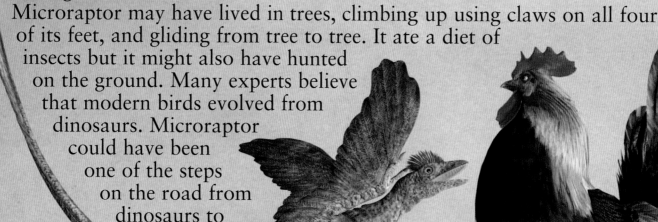

Long feathers on its rear legs would have made it tricky for Microraptor to walk and run across the ground.

Microraptor (shown with a rooster) was about 2.6 feet (0.8 m) long and weighed around 2.2 pounds (1 kg).

PROFILE: **ARCHAEOPTERYX**

Was it a bird? Was it a dinosaur? Archaeopteryx was a peculiar mixture of the two. It had some dinosaur features, and some features that modern birds have. Most experts, however, consider Archaeopteryx to be one of the earliest birds. It lived around 150 million years ago, at the same time as the dinosaurs, and was related to birdlike dinosaurs such as Velociraptor (see page 18).

Name: *Archaeopteryx*
Meaning: *First Bird*
Lived: *150–148 mya (UPPER JURASSIC)*
Fossils found: *Germany*

Mixed Features

Archaeopteryx was about the size of a crow. Like a bird, it had feathers and wings. However, it couldn't fly for more than a short hop, because it didn't have the large breastbone that is needed to support powerful flight muscles. Like many of the meat-eating dinosaurs that lived at the time, Archaeopteryx had teeth in its jaw, a long bony tail, and claws on its front limbs. Birds have none of these features.

Glider and Runner

Archaeopteryx may have climbed trees and used its simple wings to glide through the air to catch insects. But it probably caught small prey by running after it, perhaps with short flying hops.

Ten fossil skeletons of Archaeopteryx have been excavated from limestone rock in southern Germany. The rock shows patterns of the Archaeopteryx's feathers.

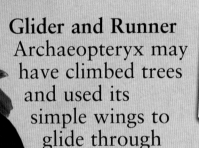

Archaeopteryx was about 1.6 feet (0.5 m) in length.

Here is Archaeopteryx and a rooster so you can compare their sizes.

FIGHT 5: MICRORAPTOR VS.

Here is a fight that never happened in real life! Microraptor and Archaeopteryx lived thirty million years apart in time and thousands of miles apart in distance. But with the aid of some super high-tech science and some fossilized DNA from each of the combatants, we have transported them to the same time and the same place.

The arena for our imaginary battle is a forest of tall conifer trees. Microraptor is perched on a branch high above the ground. Always alert, it spots an Archaeopteryx standing on a branch of a neighboring tree, just a few yards away. The Microraptor launches itself from its perch. At first it plummets toward the ground to gain speed, then spreads its four wings and glides at top speed toward the Archaeopteryx. The Archaeopteryx spots the attack, and it too takes to the air. Together, the two glide downward, twisting and turning as they try to land blows on each other. Archaeopteryx swings away and lands on a tree trunk, clinging with its claws. It begins to climb. Meanwhile, the Microraptor has fluttered to the ground. Archaeopteryx has the advantage of height. It dives down onto the Microraptor, biting its neck as it lands. Now the two fight like angry roosters. The Microraptor is more powerful, but the Archaeopteryx is more agile.

STATS
MICRORAPTOR
AKA Little Thief

STRENGTHS: Glides with four feathered limbs. Teeth and claws for attack.

WEAKNESSES: Finds it difficult to move on the ground because of large feathers.

ARCHAEOPTERYX

Feathers fly from the Microraptor's wings as the Archaeopteryx lands several bites. But then the Microraptor pins its foe down by its tail. It goes in for the kill, but Archaeopteryx wriggles free and runs. Microraptor is the winner. But it has lost its meal.

STATS

ARCHAEOPTERYX
AKA First Bird

STRENGTHS: Glides with feathered forelimbs and tail. Agile on the ground.

WEAKNESSES: Very small and lightweight.

WINNER: MICRORAPTOR

PROFILE: **TYRANNOSAURUS**

Tyrannosaurus may have been the most terrifying creature that ever lived. It was a monstrous killing machine, with the biggest mouth and the biggest teeth of any meat-eating dinosaur. No wonder it is the most famous of the dinosaurs.

Name: *Tyrannosaurus*
Meaning: *Tyrant Lizard*
Lived: *67–65 mya (UPPER CRETACEOUS)*
Fossils found: *Canada, United States*

Terrific Teeth

Tyrannosaurus was North America's top predator. It stood 19.5 feet (6 m) high and weighed more than an African elephant. Its teeth were like a mouthful of giant, curved steak knives, with serrated edges for slicing through flesh. They were curved to stop the flesh from slipping out of its mouth—a mouth that could have swallowed an adult human in one bite. A short, powerful neck allowed Tyrannosaurus to pull and twist its head to rip away the flesh from an unfortunate victim.

Tyrannosaurus had a skull 5 feet (1.5 m) long, filled with sharp teeth up to 6 inches (18 cm) long.

Big and Small

Tyrannosaurus had powerful hind legs but could not run fast.

Its forelimbs were puny—too small even to hold on to prey. It ambushed live animals when it could, but also scavenged, eating dead animals that it found.

Tyrannosaurus grew up to 39 feet (12 m) long and could weigh as much as 7.5 tons (6.8 metric tons). This fearsome predator lived mainly on horned dinosaurs, such as Triceratops, and duckbilled dinosaurs, such as Hadrosaurus.

PROFILE: SPINOSAURUS

Name: *Spinosaurus*
Meaning: *Spiny Lizard*
Lived: *95–70 mya (UPPER CRETACEOUS)*
Fossils found: *Egypt, Morocco*

Spinosaurus was an awesome creature. It had a body like a Tyrannosaurus's, a head like a giant crocodile's, and a tall, bony sail on its back. This bizarre beast was a meat-eating predator that would have topped Tyrannosaurus in a contest for size and strength. It may even have been powerful enough to tackle prey as big as the giant plant eater Diplodocus, but experts think it also hunted for fish, which it plucked from the water with its long snout.

Spinosaurus had a long, narrow skull and a jaw filled with sharp, cone-shaped teeth.

Spinosaurus's Sail

Spinosaurus had spines up to 6.5 feet (2 m) long sticking up from its backbone, covered with skin to make a sail. The sail might have been for body temperature control—for losing heat or capturing heat. It might also have been bright and colorful, and used for communicating with other dinosaurs, or in courtship displays.

Experts think that Spinosaurus walked on its two hind legs most of the time, but sometimes walked on all fours. It was probably a pretty fast runner, able to catch prey on land, and hold them in its large forelimbs.

Nobody is sure exactly how big Spinosaurus was. It grew to around 59 feet (18 m) long and weighed around 8 tons (7.2 metric tons).

Croc's Jaws

The cone-shaped teeth in Spinosaurus's upper and lower jaws interlocked when its mouth was closed. This is like a modern crocodile's jaws. Spinosaurus probably spent some time in water and some time on land.

FIGHT 6: TYRANNOSAURUS VS.

The fight everyone has been waiting for is a head-to-head between two of the fiercest dinosaurs that ever lived. In reality this fight would never have happened. Fossil evidence shows that Tyrannosaurus and Spinosaurus lived not only on different continents, but also millions of years apart in time. But here, with the aid of DNA captured from fossils, and a touch of genetic engineering, we have brought the two creatures to the African plains to meet each other.

Both the Tyrannosaurus and the Spinosaurus have sniffed the stench of rotting flesh. The smell is coming from the carcass of a Protoceratops (also created with DNA). The Tyrannosaurus finds the carcass first. It begins to feed, ripping off large chunks of rotting flesh.

The Tyrannosaurus's meal is interrupted by a terrifying roar. It looks up to see the huge Spinosaurus. The Spinosaurus hasn't eaten for days, and it's starving. Saliva dripping from its jaws, it advances toward the carcass. The two giants square up. They exchange deafening roars, each trying to frighten the other away. But neither backs down. The ground shakes as the two circle the carcass, waiting for an opportunity to attack. Suddenly the Tyrannosaurus makes a move. It lunges at the Spinosaurus. The Spinosaurus is the more agile animal. It takes a quick sideways step, but the Tyrannosaurus scores a hit, its serrated teeth ripping a gash in the Spinosaurus's neck.

STATS
TYRANNOSAURUS
AKA Tyrant Lizard

STRENGTHS: Very large and ferocious predator. Mouth lined with huge, serrated, curved teeth. Powerful jaws.

WEAKNESSES: Small, weak forelimbs.

SPINOSAURUS

STATS
SPINOSAURUS
AKA Spiny Lizard

STRENGTHS: Even bigger than Tyrannosaurus. Interlocking teeth in large jaws. Long forelimbs with sharp claws.

WEAKNESSES: Lightweight for its huge size. Mouth adapted for eating fish rather than attacking large dinosaurs.

The Tyrannosaurus's momentum carries it forward, giving the Spinosaurus the chance to counterattack. It opens a wound in the Tyrannosaurus's side with its front claws. Undeterred, the Tyrannosaurus attacks again. But it makes a mistake, and it turns out to be a fatal one. As it advances, it stumbles over the carcass of the Protoceratops. The Spinosaurus takes advantage. It sinks its teeth into the Tyrannosaurus's neck and twists its head violently from side to side, inflicting terrible damage. The Tyrant Lizard slowly collapses. The Spinosaurus has won.

WINNER: SPINOSAURUS

CREATE YOUR OWN FIGHT

You might not agree with some of the fight results in this book. If that's the case, try writing your own fight report based on the facts supplied on the prefight profile pages. Better still, choose your own dinosaurs and create your own fight.

Monster Research
Once you have chosen your two dinosaurs, do some research about them using books and the Internet. You can make them fairly similar, such as the Microraptor and the Archaeopteryx, or quite different, like the Ankylosaurus and the Triceratops.

Stats Boxes
Think about stats for each creature. Find out about any other names for the AKA section. Make a list of strengths, such as their size and how powerful they are, and if they have special features, such as sharp teeth, horns, or armor plating, and also a list of any weaknesses.

In the Ring
Pick a setting where your creatures are likely to meet, and write a blow-by-blow account of how you imagine the fight might happen. Think of each contestant's key characteristics, along with its strengths and weaknesses. Remember, there doesn't always have to be a winner.

Dinosaurs
Here is a list of some other dinosaurs that might qualify for membership in the Monster Fight Club:

Acrocanthosaurus
Allosaurus
Amargasaurus
Ceratosaurus
Deinonychus
Euoplocephalus
Majungasaurus
Pentaceratops
Shunosaurus
Stegosaurus
Suchomimus
Tarbosaurus
Titanosaurus
Torosaurus
Utahraptor

Majungasaurus may be a good dinosaur to start with. It was so ferocious that it attacked others of its own kind.

GLOSSARY

armadillo (ahr-muh-DIH-loh)
A mammal from North and South America that has a covering of strong, hard, bony plates over most of its body.

conifer (KAH-nih-fur)
An evergreen tree that has spiky needles and cones.

courtship (KORT-ship)
The time when animals look for mates so that they can breed.

DNA (DEE-en-ay)
Deoxyribonucleic acid. A material in the cells of living things that is made up of genes. Genes carry the instructions for how bodies are made and what they look like.

excavated (EK-skuh-vayt-ed)
Dug out of the ground.

fossils (FO-sulz)
The remains of long dead plants and animals that have been buried for millions of years and have turned to stone.

fused (FYOOZD)
Joined together.

herbivore (ER-buh-vor)
An animal that eats plants.

osteoderms
(OS-tee-uh-dermz)
Bony plates or scales on the skin of some animals, especially reptiles, including dinosaurs.

paleontologists
(pay-lee-on-TO-luh-jists)
Scientists who study fossils to find out more about the lives and features of extinct plants and animals.

predator (PREH-duh-ter)
An animal that hunts and kills other animals for food.

scythe (SYTH)
A tool used for cutting grass which has a long handle and a sharp, curved blade.

termite (TUR-myt)
A tiny, antlike insect.

vertebrae (VER-tuh-bray)
The bones that make up an animal's spine (backbone).

voluminous (vuh-LOO-muh-nus)
Something that is of a great size.

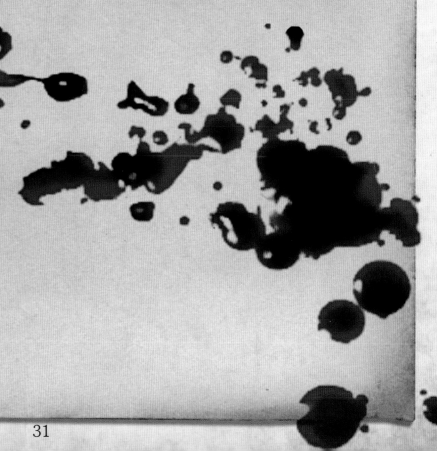

INDEX

Web Sites

Due to the changing nature of Internet links, PowerKids Press has developed an online list of Web sites related to the subject of this book. This site is updated regularly. Please use this link to access the list:
www.powerkidslinks.com/mfc/dinosaur/